THIS BOOK BELONGS TO

Steven Sharp
from
Grandma
Diehl

TELL ME
ABOUT PRAYER

By MARY ALICE JONES

Illustrated by DOROTHY GRIDER

from figures by Pelagie Doane

RAND McNALLY & COMPANY

NEW YORK   CHICAGO   SAN FRANCISCO

Acknowledgments

The following selections are used by permission of the publishers, with whom special arrangements have been made for reprinting in this book:

From *Prayers Old and New*, copyright 1935 by *The Forward Movement*, 413 Sycamore Street, Cincinnati, Ohio: "For Our Tongues," "For a Happy Home," "Make Us Sorry," "A Prayer for Every Day";

From *My Own Book of Prayers*, copyright 1938 by Rand McNally and Company: "For Courage," "I Think of God and Me," "Joy of Swift Motion," "For Trustfulness," "Some Lovely Things";

From *A Diary of Private Prayer*, by John Baillie, copyright 1936 by Charles Scribner's Sons, New York, for the United States, and by Oxford University Press, London, for the world-wide rights: "Praise to God" and "For This Day's Happiness";

From *The Temple*, by The Rev. W. E. Orchard, published and copyright by E. P. Dutton & Company, Inc., New York, and J. M. Dent & Sons, Publishers, England; copyright 1918, renewed 1946 by W. E. Orchard: "We Thank Thee."

E

CONTENTS

WHY DO WE PRAY?

BOBBY and his little sister, Mary, and his mother and John from down-the-street had just finished making taffy. They were sitting in the yard waiting for it to be ready to pull.

All of a sudden Bobby asked, "Do we *have* to say our prayers, Mother?"

His mother looked surprised. Then she smiled. "Whatever made you think of a question like that while we were making candy, Bobby?"

"I just remembered. John and I were talking about it yesterday. Do we, Mother? Do we have to?"

"No, Bobby, we do not have to. But we need to pray."

"Will God be mad at us if we don't?" John asked.

"I think not, John. But he wants us to talk with him."

"Does God really like it, Mother? To have us say our prayers, I mean?"

"I am sure he does, Bobby. You see, God loves us."

"Well, I think he would get tired of hearing the same prayer every day," John said. "I get tired of saying it."

"Do you think there is only one prayer, John? There are as many prayers as people want to make. Little children like Mary can make prayers, and bigger children like you and Bobby can make prayers, and grown people can make prayers, too."

John looked as if he did not understand. "Really? Can we make our own prayers?"

"Yes, we can. Prayers that wise and good people have made often help us say what we want to say to God. And so we learn them and use them. But when we want to, we may make our very own prayers in our very own words. The words may not be so beautiful as those in the old prayers are. But ours may be *good* prayers just the same."

"I'd like to make some new prayers," John said.

"So would I," Bobby agreed. "Will you help us, Mother? Can we make a book of prayers just for ourselves?"

Mother said she thought that was a fine plan. And so Bobby and John and Mary and some of the other children on the street made a book of prayers. They drew a cover for the book. Some of the prayers they put into their book were old, old prayers that people had prayed for years and years. Some of them were prayers other people had made. Some of them were prayers that they made themselves.

[8]

OUR OWN PRAYER BOOK

IN THE MORNING

BOBBY opened his eyes and looked out of the window. "Wake up, Mary," he called. "The sun is shining."

Mary opened her eyes. She ran to the window. "Look at Rover. He's laughing." Sure enough, their dog *was* laughing. Anyone could see that. His eyes were twinkling and his mouth was open in a friendly grin, and he was wiggling with joy.

"Hi, Rover, what are you laughing about?" Bobby called. Then Bobby laughed, too. For Rover was wagging his tail and jumping and calling, just as plainly as if he used words. "I know what he is saying," Bobby told his little sister. "He's saying, 'I'm laughing because I'm happy. Can't you see it's a sunny day?'"

"The grass is happy, too," Mary said.

Bobby thought it was silly to say the grass was happy just because it was waving in the wind. But because *he* was feeling happy, he did not tell Mary she was silly. Instead, he said, "This is such a nice day we should be good all day."

"We will make some prayers about it," Mary decided. "The way Mother said we could."

"Yes, let's," Bobby nodded. "I think God likes prayers in the morning. Then he knows we think about him the first thing when we get up."

"And he helps us all day long," Mary added.

So Bobby and Mary called their mother to help them. They found some old prayers they liked, and they made some new ones of their very own. Here are some of the morning prayers they put in their book.

MORNING PRAYERS

WHEN I WAKE UP

Dear God, when I wake up,
Let me think first of you,
And thank you for rest and sleep
In the quiet darkness
Of the night.
And thank you for work and play
That wait for me
In the light of the morning.
And thank you for
The bright and beautiful world
Into which I go.
And thank you for loving me,
Always, everywhere.

AT THE DAY'S BEGINNING

O God, who has brought us
To the beginning of this day,
Grant that this day
We fall into no sin,
Neither run into
Any kind of danger;
But that all our doing
May be right in your eyes.
—Adapted from the Book of Common Prayer

LET US WORSHIP

Let us worship and bow down:
Let us kneel before the Lord
    our Maker.
For he is our God; and we
Are his children.
Today, let us hear his voice,
And turn our hearts
    toward him.
—Adapted from Psalm 95:6-8

FOR HARD THINGS

There are hard things
That I must do today, dear God.
Hard things, but I should like
To do them well
And bravely as I can.
I ask for courage.
Let me not give up
When things go wrong,
But gladly try another way.
Dear God, be near me
Through the day
And help me do
The hard things well.
—Edith Kent Battle

[13]

TO DO WHAT I SHOULD DO

Help me this day, dear God,
To do what I should do.
To use my hands
To share with others;
To use my feet
To run swift errands;
To use my eyes
To see the beautiful world
Which you have made;
To use my mouth
For friendly words
And happy laughing all the day;
To use my mind
To think good thoughts
And learn your will for me.
Help me this day, dear God,
To do what I should do.

TO KNOW THE WAY

In the morning, O Lord,
Let me feel thy loving kindness,
For in thee do I trust:
Cause me to know the way
Wherein I should walk;
Teach me to do thy will;
For thou art my God.

—From the Psalms

A HAPPY MORNING

Thank you, dear God,
For this new day:
For its gladness
And its brightness;
For the long hours
Waiting to be filled with
Happy play and useful work.
Thank you, dear God,
For this new day.

TEACH ME

Show me thy ways, O God;
Teach me thy paths.
Lead me in thy truth,
And teach me.
On thee do I wait all the day.

—From Psalm 25:4, 5

WHEN I AM CROSS

All the creatures out-of-doors
Woke up with songs
And shouts of joy.
But I woke up all cross inside
And looking sullen-faced and sad.
Please help me, God,
To feel your love
That smooths the crossness out.

GOD'S LOVE

Thank you, God, that I can feel
Your love about me all this day;
Thank you, God, that I can know
Your thought and care
Will go with me;
Thank you, God, that I can do
The hard things
That the day may bring
Because your love and thought
Will make me strong.

GOD WILL HEAR

In the morning
I will look up to God.
God will hear me when I pray
    unto him.
God will show me what is good,
And will put gladness
    into my heart.

FOR WORDS AND THOUGHTS

Let all the words I say,
And all the thoughts of
    my heart,
Be pleasing to you,
This day, dear God.

FOR THIS DAY

O God, let each one
Who has to do with me today
Be the happier for it.
Help me every hour to know
What I should say and do,
And give me a loving heart
So that I may do
The right thing kindly.
Help me to understand
Other people,
And to know how they feel,
So that I may help them.

FOR ALL CHILDREN

Dear God, let this day
Be a happy day for children
    everywhere.
Help them all to think of you,
And of your love for them.
Help them all to be kind
To each other, and to their pets.
Let all people who take
    care of children
Be wise and loving.
Let this day be a happy day
For children everywhere.

[15]

ASKING GOD FOR WHAT WE WANT

MAY WE ask God for anything we want?" Bobby asked.

"We may talk with God about anything we wish to talk with him about, Bobby," his Mother told him. "But there are many things which I hope you will never *ask* him for."

"Why? Why shouldn't I ask him for anything I want?"

"Because some things we want are not good to want."

Just then Mary ran in. "I want a big bicycle, Mother."

Bobby laughed at her. "You couldn't ride a big bicycle, Mary. You're a little girl. You'd fall off and hurt yourself."

"But I *want* one. Ben has a big one. It goes fast."

"Yes, it does, dear," her mother agreed. "But you will have to wait until you are big like Ben is before you can ride a big bicycle."

Mary looked cross. Her mother said, "I see Susan out on the sidewalk with her tricycle. You can ride your tricycle right now."

So Mary smiled again, and went out to ride her tricycle.

"Is that what you mean about praying for something

that is not good for us?" Bobby asked. "Like Mary asking for a big bicycle?"

"That is part of it, Bobby." Then his mother went on. "There is something else we should think of, too. Sometimes we pray for what is good for us to have, but which God plans for us to get by working ourselves." And Bobby remembered about having to water his garden to get flowers.

"And sometimes," Mother added, "we pray for things that would not be *fair* for us to have. We ask for more than our share, and do not think about what somebody else may need."

"Like wanting ice cream when somebody else hasn't had any milk?" Bobby asked. "My teacher said we did that."

"Something like that, son. And sometimes we try to get our own way by asking God to make everything go just the way we want it to go."

"Like asking him always to let us win a game?"

"Yes, Bobby," his mother said. "And sometimes we even ask God to hurt somebody else so we can have what we want."

"That would not be good," Bobby agreed. "What kind of prayers should we make, Mother? How should we pray for what we want?"

And so Bobby's mother helped him make some prayers about the things he wanted.

PRAYERS FOR WHAT I WANT

GIVE WHAT WE NEED

Give us this day
Our daily bread,
We pray, dear God, our Father.
And all we need
To make us grow
And keep us strong
And healthy:
Clothes to warm us
On wintry days,
And a house to give us
        shelter;
Good books to read,
And a place to play
And work in.
Give us, dear God,
The things we need,
To make us strong and good.

IN JESUS' NAME

I would remember Jesus
When I pray, dear God.
And I would make my prayer
In his dear name.
He asked not for
Special favors
And gifts he did not need.
And so I pray that I may be
Unselfish in the prayers
I make.
He loved all men,
And so I pray
That I may love them, too.
He prayed to know
Your will for him;
And so I pray that I may know
What you would have me do.

NOT TOO MUCH

Dear God,
Let me not ask for too much,
Or want always to get
The best for myself.

Dear God, let me remember
That others need things, too,
And so be willing to share
The good things I want.

[19]

THINGS I WANT

I want so many things,
Dear God!
I want a bicycle and a bat;
I want a football
And a chest of tools;
I want some books
And a trip to camp.
I want so many things,
Dear God!
Please help me not to want
Too much,
Nor ask for more
Than my share.
Please help me to like
The things I have
And be happy
Without all I want.

GOD'S PLAN

Father God,
I trust your love,
And know that what you plan
For me is good.
Please help me learn
To work with you and carry out
Your plans for me.

PRAYER AND WORK

When I pray for good things
For myself and for my friends,
Please help me, God,
        to remember
That I have a part to do,
And let me work
The best I can
To help you give me
The good things
That I pray for.

IF IT IS GOOD

If it is good for me
        to have it,
Please let me have a pet,
        dear God.
I know it means
        a lot of work,
And remembering every day
To feed it and bathe it,
And keep it from bothering
        the neighbors.
But if it is good for me
        to have it,
Please let me have a pet,
        dear God.

GIVE WHAT IS BEST

You are wise, dear God,
And know my needs before I ask.
Give me what is best for me.
And when I ask
For that which is not good,
Give me understanding
That I may know what is right.
And when I ask
For that which may not be,
Let me trust your love.

WHAT IS GOOD

Help me to want what is good,
    dear God,
And to know what I should
    pray for.
Help me to think of what
    I can do
To make the good that I want
    come true.

MANY THINGS TO DO

The world is full of pleasant
Things to do each day.
Please help me, God, to choose
To do the things that are good.

BECAUSE GOD LOVES ME

You love me, God,
And so you want
To help me to be happy.
Please let me think
Of what is good
And right for me to do.
Please let me think
Of pleasant ways to play
And work and live with others.

HELP MY TEAM

Dear God, help my team.
Help it be a good team,
And help it play a good game.
Let nobody want to win
    so much
That he forgets to play fairly.
Help the other team, too.
Help it to play a good game.
Let the team that loses
Be a good loser,
And let the team that wins
Be a good winner.
Help my team to be
A *good* team,
Dear God.

GOD HEARS OUR PRAYERS

BOBBY and his daddy had been to the fair. They had a fine time watching the people and the animals and the acrobats. But Bobby was glad to go home when it was over.

"The fair was fun, Daddy, but there were too many people.

"Don't you like crowds, son?"

"Not such *big* crowds."

That night when Bobby was ready for bed, his daddy came to say good night. "Daddy, I've been wondering about so many people. Like at the fair. How does God hear all of them? When they say their prayers, I mean."

"He is God, Bobby. He is great beyond our knowing. But he loves us, too. That is why he hears all of us."

"How does God have enough love for everybody?"

"There is something strange about love, son. When you divide an apple, the halves are less than the whole apple. But when you divide love, it seems to grow bigger."

Bobby looked as if he did not understand; so his daddy went on.

"Once, you know, Mother and I had only one child—Bobby. We gave him all the love we had. Then we had another child—Mary. But we didn't have to take away love from Bobby to have some for Mary. We found that we had *more* love. We had plenty of love for Bobby and Mary."

Bobby understood about that. He knew his mother and daddy did not take away love from him to give to Mary.

Then he laughed. "Mr. and Mrs. Thompson must have lots and lots of love, because they have seven children."

His daddy laughed, too.

"I am sure they have plenty of love for all of them."

Bobby and his daddy were quiet a moment, thinking.

"And God isn't too busy to listen when we all pray?" Bobby asked.

"It is one of the most wonderful thoughts in the world, son, that he isn't too busy. That the great God who made the mountains and the waterfalls and the sun and the stars loves each one of us and hears us when we pray."

"You know, Daddy, I like to think about that. Of everybody being a big family and God having enough love and listening. Like Mr. and Mrs. Thompson and seven children, only lots more." He nodded his head. "Yes, I like that. Now I'll say my prayers with all the people round the world."

PRAYERS TO HELP US LISTEN

WHEREVER I AM

Wherever I am, dear God,
I can pray to you:
In the church,
Or along the highway.
Whatever I do, dear God,
I can pray to you:
If I eat my food,
Or help my father;
If I go to ride,
Or play with my friends;
If I read a book,
Or use my tools.
Wherever I am, whatever I do,
I can pray to you, dear God.

GOD LOVES US

Behold what manner of love
The Father hath bestowed
        upon us,
That we should be called
The sons of God.
Beloved,
Let us love one another.
—*From the Epistles*

ALL CHILDREN

I pray
That all the children, God,
Of this great wide, wide world
May know of your dear love
        for them,
And of your plan that they
Should love each other, too,
And work together, every one,
To do your will on earth.

GOD CARES

O God, I love to think
How great you are,
And yet how you can be
        my friend.
I think of you
        as making worlds,
Yet caring what I do!
When I have done my best
I think I feel nearer to you—
Yet, when I am puzzled, bad,
        or sad,
I feel you near me, too.
—*Jeanette Perkins Brown*

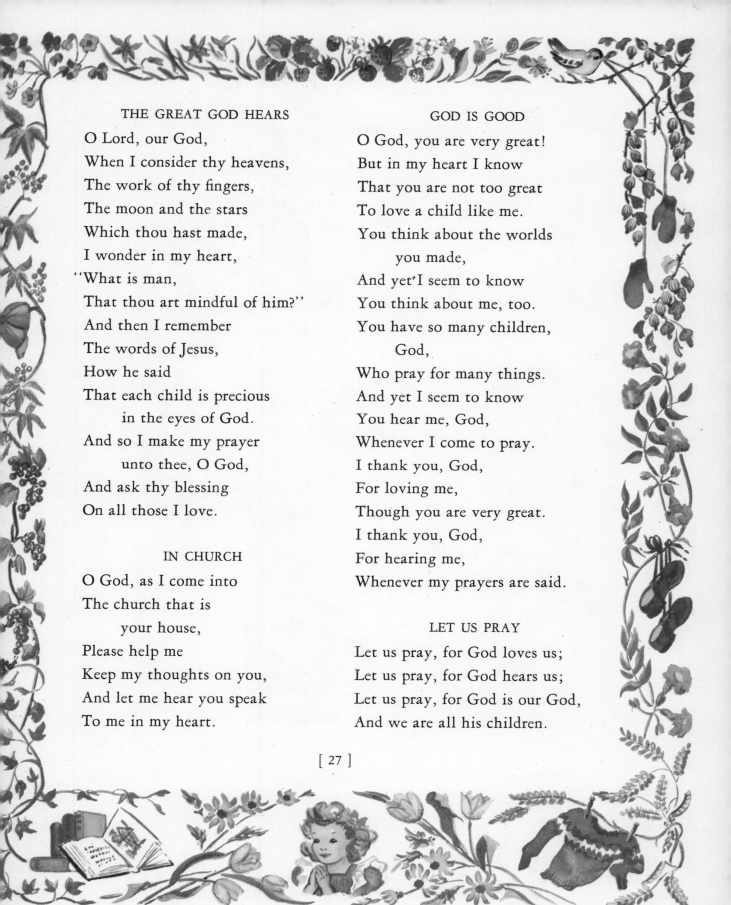

THE GREAT GOD HEARS

O Lord, our God,
When I consider thy heavens,
The work of thy fingers,
The moon and the stars
Which thou hast made,
I wonder in my heart,
"What is man,
That thou art mindful of him?"
And then I remember
The words of Jesus,
How he said
That each child is precious
    in the eyes of God.
And so I make my prayer
    unto thee, O God,
And ask thy blessing
On all those I love.

IN CHURCH

O God, as I come into
The church that is
    your house,
Please help me
Keep my thoughts on you,
And let me hear you speak
To me in my heart.

GOD IS GOOD

O God, you are very great!
But in my heart I know
That you are not too great
To love a child like me.
You think about the worlds
    you made,
And yet I seem to know
You think about me, too.
You have so many children,
    God,
Who pray for many things.
And yet I seem to know
You hear me, God,
Whenever I come to pray.
I thank you, God,
For loving me,
Though you are very great.
I thank you, God,
For hearing me,
Whenever my prayers are said.

LET US PRAY

Let us pray, for God loves us;
Let us pray, for God hears us;
Let us pray, for God is our God,
And we are all his children.

WHEN WE DO NOT GET
WHAT WE PRAY FOR

I'M NOT going to pray any more," Bobby announced.

His mother looked at him. "Aren't you, son?"

"Just look at that rain," Bobby went on. "I asked God to send a nice day today for the school trip. I asked him two nights. And he didn't."

"Is that why you pray, Bobby? To tell God what he should do?"

Bobby thought a minute. Then he looked uncomfortable.

"That doesn't sound right, does it? That I should tell God what to do?"

"Not if you trust God, son. This is a very great world. There is a great deal about it that we have not learned to understand. We might make some bad mistakes if God let us tell him what to do."

"But I did want a nice holiday, " Bobby said.

"I know you did. And I wanted a nice holiday for you.

[29]

And I think God, too, is sorry you are disappointed about the trip. But God has many things to think about as he hears all our prayers. Right this minute I know some people are *glad* it is raining. I think they are saying, 'Thank God for the rain,' because their fields need rain to make the grain grow. Daddy said just yesterday that our garden needed rain."

"But we could water it," Bobby said.

"Yes, we could. And in some places men have learned how to water all the big fields whenever they need water."

"I saw some pictures of it," Bobby remembered. "They make ditches and run water to the fields."

"And men are learning how to make dams to keep the rain from causing floods, and to store up the rain when we have a lot of it so we can use it when we need it. We may learn how to use the rain in better ways, but we could not get along without it."

Bobby thought some more. "Then shouldn't I ask God for a nice day? Not ever?"

"You can always talk with God about whatever you want to talk with him about, Bobby. But I think it is not good to tell God what to do, and be angry when he does not do it. I think it is better to ask God to help us to know what he wants us to do with what we have."

"Will he help us to learn how to make it stop raining?" Bobby wanted to know.

His mother laughed. "Well, I am not sure about that. Though some people are trying to find ways of making it rain in one place and stopping rain in another. But one thing we can be sure of. If we ask God to help us to understand our world, we will be ready to learn more and more about the rules it goes by. And we will be able to learn how to use the rules in good ways."

"Tell me how I should pray about things like that. What should I say, Mother?"

So Bobby and his mother made some prayers for talking with God about understanding the world.

PRAYERS FOR UNDERSTANDING

GOD MADE THE WORLD

Dear God, you have made
    the world,
For you are very great.
And you made me to be your child,
For you are loving, too.
Help me to understand
The world that you have planned,
And learn to make it good.
Help me to know your laws
And keep them every day.

A RAINY DAY

On a dull, rainy day
That keeps me indoors
And makes my good plans
All go wrong,
Please help me, dear God,
To be cheerful and gay.
Help me to think of other plans
To keep me busy, happy, and glad,
So I can say,
"Thank God for the rain!"

WHEN I DON'T UNDERSTAND

There are so many things, dear God,
That I don't understand!
Why is it there are
Droughts and floods,
And storms upon the sea?
Why is it the brooks run dry
And little flowers die of thirst?
Why is it that
Some boys and girls
Are always hungry, never warm?
I think you know the reason

Why these things
Are just the way they are.
I wonder—
Will you help me, God,
To understand them, too?
I wonder—
Can I help you, God,
Some day when I am wise,
To stop the droughts
And storms and floods
And give all children food?

MAN'S POWER

We thank you, O God,
For all the power
You have given to men;
That they may learn
To build bridges
    over rushing rivers,
And fly airplanes
    through the sky;
That they may plant wheat fields
And find oil in the earth;
That they may paint pictures
    and make lovely music;
That they may understand
    your laws
And learn to live together
    as brothers.
We thank you, O God,
For all the power
You have given to man.

FOR ALL SWIFT MOTION

O God, giver of all
That makes us glad,
We bring you praise
For all swift motion:
For blowing wind,
And rippling, flowing water;
For the flying birds;
For planes that follow
The airways above us;
For the moving of fish
    in the stream;
For the power of motion
    in our limbs,
The power to run and leap
And dance and swim.
O God, giver of all
That makes us glad,
We bring you praise
For all swift motion.

—*Edith Kent Battle*

TEACH ME

Teach me, O God;
Give me understanding,
And I will keep your law.

—*Psalm 119:34*

ASKING GOD FOR
FORGIVENESS AND HELP

BOBBY was walking home by himself, feeling mad all over.

"Hello, son. All by yourself this afternoon?"

Bobby looked up and saw his daddy opening the door of the car. "Jump in. I have to see a man out in the country, and I thought I would pick up some of you boys. But I find nobody except you." Daddy smiled as if he knew something was wrong, and Bobby got in the car.

"Everybody was mean to me today," Bobby began, as they started off. "I'm glad the other boys won't get a ride."

"Are you?" Daddy asked. "You might have had more fun with them."

"I don't *want* them," Bobby insisted. "They are mean."

His daddy didn't say anything, so Bobby had time to think. He began to wish the other boys had come. He remembered that the trouble hadn't been all their fault.

"I quarrelled with the others," he told his daddy. "They

wouldn't do what I wanted to do, and I got mad at them."

"People often quarrel about having their own way, son."

"It was silly, though," Bobby went on. "I acted like a baby. I threw dirt at them and wouldn't play."

"It is good to know it was silly, Bobby. Maybe next time you will remember it is silly *before* you do it."

"Will God be mad at me for doing it?" Bobby asked.

"No, son. I think God does not get mad with us the way we get mad with one another. But when we break his rules for living we are unhappy."

"Like not having the boys with us now?"

His daddy smiled, "Yes, something like this usually happens. The other boys did not get the ride which they would have liked. And you did not have the fun of playing in the country with them, which you would have liked."

"Will God help me to remember next time if I ask him?"

"I am sure he will, son. He forgives us when we do what is bad and are sorry. And he helps us to do what is good. I think none of us could get along without praying to God to forgive us and help us."

"Tell me how to pray about it," Bobby asked.

And so his daddy helped him make some prayers about being sorry and about remembering to be good.

PRAYERS FOR FORGIVENESS AND HELP

FOR A GENTLE HEART

Give me, dear God,
    a gentle heart
Toward all things that live:
The little creatures
    of the air,
The little creatures
    of the earth,
And all the flowers
    and the trees.
Let me not hurt them,
Nor carelessly destroy
The life that you have made.

FOR OUR TONGUES

O God, keep us free
From all untrue and
    unkind words;
Help us to use the gift
    of speech
To help others
And to give thanks to you
For all your goodness to us.
Keep us sometimes quiet
    and silent,
That our hearts and our minds
May listen to your voice.
—Prayers Old and New

FOR A HAPPY HOME

O loving Father,
Bless our home,
That we may all be happy
    in your love,
And in our love for each other.
Make us loyal and generous,
Ready to help and quick
    to forgive,
Sharing our joys

And comforting our sorrows.
May your loving spirit
Rule our hearts and lips
By the law of kindness.
O loving Father,
Make us all
Your true and happy children,
And fill our home
With the gladness of your presence.
—Prayers Old and New

[37]

HELP ME, GOD

Help me, dear God, to remember
That I am your child,
And belong to you.
Help me to love others
As you have loved me.
Help me to be generous and kind,
Truthful in what I say,
And kind to those about me.
Speak to my mind,
That I may know you;
Speak to my heart,
That I may love you;
Speak to my body, that it may do
What you would have me do.

MAKE US SORRY

O God, make us sorry
For all the wrong things
We have done.
Keep us from all meanness
And selfishness,
And from hurting others by
What we say or what we do.
Help us gladly to obey
Our parents and teachers;
Make us careful and cheerful
In doing every duty.
Help us to be truthful and honest,
And let us know you better
And love you more every day.

A PRAYER FOR EVERY DAY

O God, give me clean hands,
Clean words,
Clean thoughts.
Help me to stand
For the hard right
Against the easy wrong.
Save me from habits
That hurt me and others.
Teach me to work as hard
And play as fair
In your sight alone
As if the whole world saw.
Forgive me when I am unkind,
And help me to forgive those
Who are unkind to me.
Keep me ready to help others
At some cost to myself.
Send me chances
To do some good every day,
And so grow more like Jesus.

—Prayers Old and New

[38]

I HAVE DONE WRONG

Forgive me, God,
For all I have spoken falsely
Or in anger;
Forgive me for doing wrong
When I have known a better way;
Forgive me for forgetting
When I could have remembered.
Forgive me, God,
Because you love me.

HELP ME TO LOVE

Help me, God, to love
Those who do not love me,
And those who are unkind;
Remembering Jesus,
Who loved his enemies
And those who hurt him.

FOR FORGIVENESS

O God, you know my foolishness;
And my sins are not hidden
        from thee.
Hear me as I pray,
For thou, O God, art good,
And ready to forgive.
        —*Adapted from Psalms 29:5; 86:5*

FOR TRUSTFULNESS

Our Father,
Teach us not to fear,
Since thou, dear God,
Art always near.
And though no friend
Be at our side,
Thou art our ever certain
        guide.
Teach us to trust
Thy loving care,
All times and places—
        everywhere.
        —*Edith Kent Battle*

GOD IS NEAR

My help comes from God,
Who made heaven and earth.
God will not forget me.
The great God,
Who never slumbers nor sleeps,
Will be my helper.
He will keep me from evil.
He will keep my going out
And my coming in
This day and every day.
        —*Adapted from Psalm 121*

[39]

PRAISING GOD
AND THANKING HIM

MARY was out in the front yard. The wind was blowing softly. She stood still and let the wind blow in her face. She skipped and let the wind chase her and toss her hair.

"The wind is playing with me," she called as her mother came out of the house. "It blew my hair and chased me."

"The wind can be a jolly playmate," Mother said. "Look, it is playing with the flowers, too."

Just then they saw Bobby coming home from school.

His mother waved to him, as he came running toward them. "Did you have a good day at school, son?"

"Yes, I did. We learned about farms and we went to see a big one. There were wheat fields and vegetable gardens and fruit trees and chickens and cows."

"What a lot of good food you saw growing!"

"Yes, I thought about that."

"Come play with me," Mary called. As Bobby and Mary

began running in the wind, Rover came dashing after them. When he stopped suddenly, Bobby looked up. John and his dog Samson were on the sidewalk.

"Hi, John! Bring Samson over to play," Bobby called.

"May I ask Susan to bring Ginger?" Mary asked. "It will be fun to have lots of dogs." Her mother thought so, too; so Bobby and John and Mary and Susan and the dogs had a good time playing in the yard.

When John and Susan had gone home to supper, Bobby said, "It's fun having pets and friends to play with."

"And to have the wind to play with," Mary added.

"It's been a nice day, Mother," Bobby went on. "There was the farm and the food growing and everything."

"I am glad you had a good day," Mother said. "I have been happy, too. I think I should like to tell God about it."

"Is that a good way to pray, Mother? Just to tell God we are happy? And not ask for anything?"

"I am sure it is, Bobby. To tell God how glad we are that he made so beautiful a world for us to live in. And to thank him for food and friends and families and pets to enjoy."

"I think I would like to pray that way," Bobby said. And so Bobby and Mary and their mother made some prayers of thanks and praise.

PRAYERS OF PRAISE AND THANKSGIVING

PRAISE TO GOD

Now unto thee, O God,
Be all praise and glory,
That day by day
Thou dost richly fill my life
With various blessings:
A home to share,
Kindred to love,
And friends to cherish:
A place to fill and work to do:
A green world to live in,
Blue skies above me,
And pure air to breathe:
Healthy exercise
And simple pleasures:
Good books to read
And many arts and crafts
To delight in:
So much that is worth knowing
And skill and science to know it:
Many happy days,
And that inward calm
That thou givest me
In days of gloom.

—*John Baillie*

FOR CHRISTMAS

We thank you, God,
For this happy day.
We thank you for the love
   in our homes,
And for the love of friends.
Most of all, dear God,
We thank you for sending Jesus
   into the world
To show all men everywhere
Your love for them.
Help us today
To remember Jesus,
And to show our love for him
By living happily
     with one another,
And in good will with
All your children everywhere.

LET ME KNOW YOUR GOODNESS

Let me know your goodness, God,
As I eat my daily food;
Let me feel your love
As I enjoy my world.

[43]

WE THANK THEE

We thank thee, dear God,
For the gladness
    of the morning,
For the freedom of the wind,
The music of the rain,
The joy of the sunshine,
And the deep calm of the night;
For trees and flowers
    and clouds and skies,
For the tender ministries
    of human love,
The unselfishness of parents,
For the patience of teachers,
And the encouragement
    of friends.

—W. E. Orchard*

GRACE BEFORE MEALS

The eyes of all
Wait upon thee, O Lord:
And thou giveth them meat
In due season.
Bless, O Lord, this food
    to our use,
And us to thy service,
And make us ever mindful
Of the needs of others.

THANKS BE TO GOD

Thanks be to God
For the good world
    he has made:
For earth and sea and sky;
For sun and moon and stars;
For daylight and darkness;
For summer and winter;
Seedtime and harvest.
Thanks be to God
For streams of sparkling
    water;
For wind and rain
    and snowflakes;
For trees and grass
    and flowers;
For cattle, sheep, and horses;
For singing birds and
Playful pets.
Thanks be to God
For work and play and worship;
For home, friends, and teachers;
For music, books, and pictures;
For health, joy, and laughter.
Thanks be to God
For the good world
    he has made.

[44]

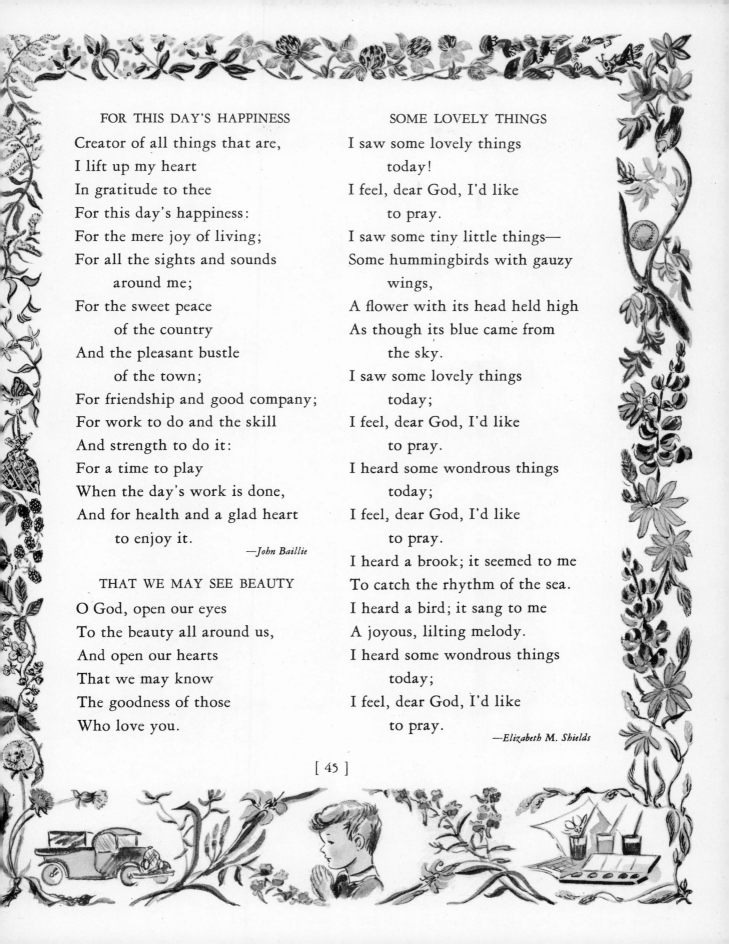

FOR THIS DAY'S HAPPINESS

Creator of all things that are,
I lift up my heart
In gratitude to thee
For this day's happiness:
For the mere joy of living;
For all the sights and sounds
  around me;
For the sweet peace
  of the country
And the pleasant bustle
  of the town;
For friendship and good company;
For work to do and the skill
And strength to do it:
For a time to play
When the day's work is done,
And for health and a glad heart
  to enjoy it.
    —*John Baillie*

THAT WE MAY SEE BEAUTY

O God, open our eyes
To the beauty all around us,
And open our hearts
That we may know
The goodness of those
Who love you.

SOME LOVELY THINGS

I saw some lovely things
  today!
I feel, dear God, I'd like
  to pray.
I saw some tiny little things—
Some hummingbirds with gauzy
  wings,
A flower with its head held high
As though its blue came from
  the sky.
I saw some lovely things
  today;
I feel, dear God, I'd like
  to pray.
I heard some wondrous things
  today;
I feel, dear God, I'd like
  to pray.
I heard a brook; it seemed to me
To catch the rhythm of the sea.
I heard a bird; it sang to me
A joyous, lilting melody.
I heard some wondrous things
  today;
I feel, dear God, I'd like
  to pray.
    —*Elizabeth M. Shields*

PRAYING FOR OTHERS
WHO NEED HELP

BOBBY and Mary and their mother and daddy were coming home from their church. A visitor had been there. He had told the people about some children who were hungry and cold and sick. All the people at church had prayed that God would help the children.

"Why do we pray to God to take care of the children?" Bobby asked. "I should think he would *want* to do it."

"That isn't really what we prayed for, son," his daddy said. "Do you remember? We prayed that the children would know God was loving them. We prayed that God would help us to want to share with them."

Bobby remembered. "But why do *we* have to take care of them? Why doesn't God do it?" he wanted to know.

"Would you like to live in a world where people did not love each other and help each other, Bobby? Where there were no kind people to help sick children be well? Would

[47]

it be a good world if nobody thought of anybody else? But everybody thought only of what he wanted and of how to get his own way?"

Bobby thought about that for a minute. "And nobody took turns or gave presents or shared? No, that would not be a good world," he decided.

"God knew when he planned our world that people would not be happy unless they thought of each other and helped each other. And so he planned it that way."

"Tell me more about it."

"He left some things for people to do for each other. Mothers and fathers and teachers and doctors to help boys and girls, and boys and girls to share with one another. And people in all nations to help each other. If people are selfish or mean, others suffer. That is the way the world is made."

Bobby thought some more. "And if we pray, does God make us remember to help other people? Is that the way he takes care of them?"

"That is not the only way God takes care of them, Bobby, but it is one important way. When we pray for other people, God helps us to think of ways we can help them. He helps doctors to think of ways to take care of children. And he helps the people we pray for to be better because they feel that we love them and are praying for them."

"I think God has helped us to know ways we can help take care of the children we heard about at church," Mother said. "I know we could send them some cereal."

"And I could send them one of my sweaters," Bobby said.

"I could send them one of my sweaters, too," Mary said.

"And I could take some money out of the bank and give it to the man to buy some milk for them," Daddy said.

"But the man said there were so many children," Bobby remembered. "I think we should ask God to help lots and lots of people to want to send them something."

"And to help the children to know that he loves them always," Mother added.

"And to help the children to know that we love them, too," Mary said.

So they prayed for the children who were hungry and cold and sick. And they made some prayers for other people who needed help, too.

PRAYERS FOR OTHERS

THE WORKERS OF THE WORLD

Dear God, I pray
For the workers of the world:
For those who care for animals
And those who grow our food;
For those who mine the coal
And those who run the trains;
For those who buy and sell
And those who keep the house;
For those who tend the sick
And those who keep us well;
For those whose work
    is dangerous
And those whose work is dull.
Dear God, I pray
For the workers of the world.

FOR A SICK FRIEND

O God, I come to you for help.
Take care of one I love
    who is sick.
Show the doctors who come
What will help him most.
Let the nurses
Who take care of him
Be kind and gentle and skillful.
Let those who are anxious
    about him
Be brave and strong
    and unafraid.
Give him courage
When the pain hurts,
And help him to get well.

FOR FRIENDLY FOLK

We thank you, God,
For all the friendly people
Whom we have met this day.
We thank you for their
    kindness
Which has made us glad.

We thank you for their joy
Which has brought us
    good cheer.
We send them thoughts of love
And pray that we may always
Have them for our friends.

THOSE WHO NEED HELP

Dear God, I would think
    of other children
To whom this morning's light
Brings less joy than it brings
    to me:
Of those who must lie in bed
While I can run and shout;
Of those whose eyes are blind
    and cannot see;
Of those who are far away
    from their homes;
Of those who wake up shivering
And hungry and afraid.
Help them to know
That you love them, God,
And that I love them, too.

FOR THOSE WHO ARE SAD

O God, who never sleeps
And never is tired,
Be close this night
To those who are sad.
Let them feel your love,
And know that in this world
Other people are thinking of them.

FOR GOOD PEOPLE

Thank you, God,
For all good people:
For people who are strong
    and brave
When others are afraid;
For people who help others
To be happy and good;
For people who are cheerful
When things go wrong.
Thank you, God,
For all good people.

FOR THE UNTAUGHT

I would pray, dear God,
For those who have never
    been taught;
For the children who have
    never heard
Of your dear love for them,
Nor of the way you would
Have them live together.
Send them teachers, God,
Teachers who will love them
And show them
What is good.

PRAYING TO LEARN
GOD'S PLAN FOR US

BOBBY and his mother and daddy and Mary had gone to the seashore for a vacation. One day Bobby was reading a paper his teacher at church had sent him. He read, "God knows what you have need of before you ask him."

"Is that true, Mother?" Bobby wanted to know.

"Yes, I think that is true, Bobby."

"Then why do we say our prayers? Why should we tell him when he knows already?"

"Let me ask you another question, Bobby. Do Mother and Daddy know what food is good for you to eat, and do they plan it for you?"

Bobby nodded his head. His mother went on.

"But what would happen if you didn't eat the good food?"

"I would not grow. I would be hungry."

"It is something like that with praying, son. God plans for us to have the things that are best for us and to live the way that is best for us. But if we do not know what he plans for us, we often get into trouble. Or we do not get something good that God would like for us to have. Or we do not do something good that God would like for us to do. So we need to talk things over with God."

"Like with you and Daddy?" Bobby asked.

"Something like that, Bobby. God is very great. We do not understand all about his plans for us. But if we talk things over with him, he can help us understand."

"How does he? How does he help us know?"

"Some good ideas which we had never thought of, we will think of. Some good ways of doing things that we had never tried, we will decide to try. Some good plans which we had never made, we will make."

"I thought praying was telling God about things," Bobby said. "Is it letting God tell us about things?"

"I think God wants us to tell him everything we want to tell him, Bobby. But sometimes we are so busy telling God things that we do not stop to listen. He wants us to listen, too. There is so much we need to know."

"Yes, I think it would be good to listen," Bobby agreed. "Show me how to pray a listening prayer."

And so Bobby and his mother prayed a listening prayer.

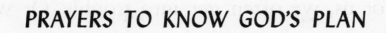

PRAYERS TO KNOW GOD'S PLAN

GOD LOVES US

Let us think how much
God has loved us!
He has called us his children.
He has sent his Son, Jesus,
Into the world
To show us his love.
Because God so loved us,
Let us love one another.

SPEAK TO ME, GOD

Speak to me, God,
And let me be quiet and listen.
Speak to me, God,
And let me know your way.
Speak to me, God,
And let me do your will.

I WILL BE STILL

I will be still,
That I may know God is here;
I will hear
What the Lord will speak.

TEACH ME THY WAY

Teach me thy way, O Lord;
I will walk in thy truth:
For thou art great
And doest wondrous things.
Thou art God alone.

—From the Psalms

OPEN MY MIND

Thank God for my mind,
For I can think and plan
　　and understand.
I can choose
And know the reason
　　for my choice.
Help me, dear God,
To open my mind
To all that you would teach me.
Help me, God,
That I may learn
Of your great love and plan;
Of your great wisdom,
Power, and might,
Which made our world and me.

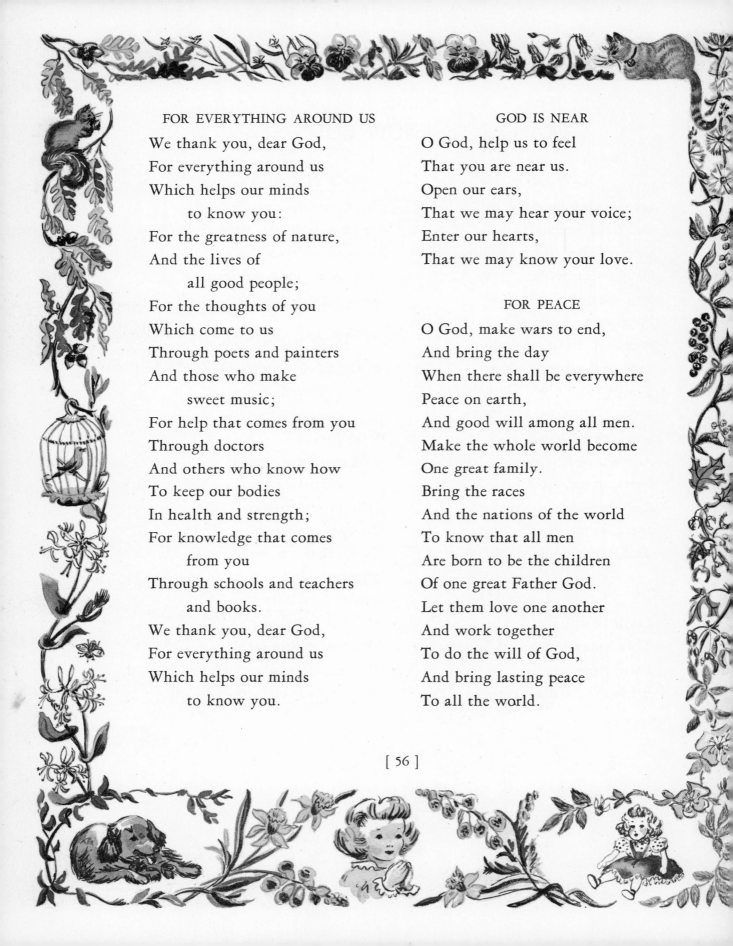

FOR EVERYTHING AROUND US

We thank you, dear God,
For everything around us
Which helps our minds
    to know you:
For the greatness of nature,
And the lives of
    all good people;
For the thoughts of you
Which come to us
Through poets and painters
And those who make
    sweet music;
For help that comes from you
Through doctors
And others who know how
To keep our bodies
In health and strength;
For knowledge that comes
    from you
Through schools and teachers
    and books.
We thank you, dear God,
For everything around us
Which helps our minds
    to know you.

GOD IS NEAR

O God, help us to feel
That you are near us.
Open our ears,
That we may hear your voice;
Enter our hearts,
That we may know your love.

FOR PEACE

O God, make wars to end,
And bring the day
When there shall be everywhere
Peace on earth,
And good will among all men.
Make the whole world become
One great family.
Bring the races
And the nations of the world
To know that all men
Are born to be the children
Of one great Father God.
Let them love one another
And work together
To do the will of God,
And bring lasting peace
To all the world.

LET US HEAR

O God, you have planned,
For those who love you,
Good things that we
Do not dream of.
Keep us from thinking
So much about what we want
That we do not listen
To hear what you would
        tell us.

GOD BLESS OUR COUNTRY

God bless our country!
Help all the people
To be good people.
Help them to elect good leaders,
And help the leaders
To be fair and wise and brave.
Help fathers and mothers
And all the children
To make our country
A land of happy homes.
Help all the workers
And the people who manage money
To be honest and thoughtful
Of the happiness of others.
God bless our country!

GOD'S WAY BE KNOWN

God be merciful unto us,
        and bless us,
And cause his face to
        shine upon us;
That thy ways may be known
        upon earth,
Thy saving health among
        all nations.
Let the people praise thee,
        O God;
Let all the people praise thee.
Oh, let the nations be glad
        and sing for joy;
For thou shalt judge the people
        righteously,
And govern the nations
        upon earth.
Let the people praise thee,
        O God,
Let all the people praise thee.
Then shall the earth yield
        her increase:
And God, even our own God,
        shall bless us,
And all the ends of the earth
Shall fear him.

—From Psalm 67

PRAYER IN TIME OF TROUBLE

BOBBY and John and Rover had gone to the little wood near their houses to play. As they were about ready to start home, Rover saw something near the creek. He ran toward it. Bobby raced with him.

"Bring Rover back, Bobby," John called. "He's going too near the creek."

"We're not too near the creek," Bobby called back.

But as Rover barked and ran in and out among the tall grasses he came nearer and nearer to the creek bank. Then it happened! Rover's foot caught on a root and over he went, *splash,* into the creek.

"Run and get Mother," Bobby shouted to John. Then he held tightly to a bush and saw Rover bobbing around in the water. "Swim, Rover! Swim!" he called. But Rover did not know how to swim very well.

Bobby was afraid. He thought of God. "Please, God, don't let Rover drown. Send Mother quick. *Don't* let Rover drown."

Just then Ben, a big boy who lived in the next block,

came along through the woods with his dog, Blitz.

"Anything wrong, Bobby?" Then he saw what had happened. "Come on, Blitz, let's go after Rover."

And soon a dripping Rover was safe on the ground.

Bobby hugged Rover to get him warm. "Thank you, Ben," he said. "I asked for Mother, but he sent you. I guess you were nearer."

Ben did not know what Bobby meant. "Nobody sent me," he said. "Blitz and I were just taking a walk. I'm glad we saw you and Rover. So long, now." And he and Blitz started off.

In a minute Mother and John came running. When Mother saw Bobby and Rover safe on the ground, she stopped and leaned against a tree.

"God sent Ben and Blitz to get Rover out," Bobby explained. "It is a good thing I thought about praying. God answered in a hurry."

Mother thought a minute.

"I'm so glad and thankful that Ben and Blitz came, Bobby," she said. "But you know sometimes when we pray

for help it does not come just the way we want it to."

"Even when we ask God to send somebody?"

"Even when we pray just as you prayed about Rover."

"But if God doesn't take care of us when we ask him to, why do we say prayers?" John asked. "Doesn't he listen?"

"Yes, John. I think God always listens. And he helps us. He helps us to use our minds and know how to keep out of danger. He helps us to know what to do when we are in danger. And if we do get hurt, he helps us to be brave."

"I would like it better if he always sent someone," Bobby said.

"So would I, and so would most people, son. But remember always that God *does* help us whenever we pray for help, even though we do suffer."

Bobby was thinking. "Does everybody ask God to help him when he is in trouble? Like with Rover, I mean. And when people are sick."

"Not everybody, but I think most people do."

"What kind of prayers do they say? Do we know them?"

"Some of the prayers others have prayed in trouble have been kept for us. We can make prayers of our own, too."

"Let's do that," Bobby said. "I think it helps to pray when you are in trouble."

PRAYERS IN TROUBLE

THE LORD IS MY SHEPHERD

The Lord is my shepherd;
I shall not want.
He maketh me to lie down
In green pastures;
He leadeth me beside
    the still waters.
He restoreth my soul:
He leadeth me in the
    path of righteousness
For his name's sake.
Yea, though I walk through
The valley of the shadow of death,
I will fear no evil; for thou
Art with me; thy rod and thy staff,
They comfort me.
Thou preparest a table before me
In the presence of mine enemies:
Thou anointest my head with oil;
My cup runneth over.
Surely goodness and mercy shall
Follow me all the days of my life;
And I will dwell in the house
    of the Lord forever.
—Psalm 23

BE NOT AFRAID

I will give thanks unto thee,
O God, for thou comfortest me.
I will trust and not be afraid,
For God is my strength.
—Adapted from Isaiah 12:1, 2

IN SUNSHINE OR RAIN

Whether you send sunshine
Or whether you send rain,
Let me be glad, dear God,
And trust your love.

IN AN ACCIDENT

Dear God, there has been
An accident, and I am afraid.
Please make me brave,
And let me use my mind
To remember all I have learned
About what to do
In case of accident.
Please help me know
What I should do right now.
I know you will help me, God,
And so I will be brave.

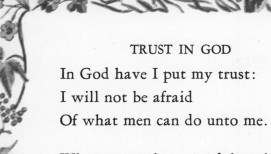

TRUST IN GOD

In God have I put my trust:
I will not be afraid
Of what men can do unto me.

Who among the sons of the mighty
Can be likened unto the Lord?
In his hands are
The deep places of the earth.
The strength of the hills
    is his also;
The sea is his, and he made it;
And his hands formed
The dry land.

Who among the sons of the mighty
Can be likened unto the Lord?
God will judge the world
    with righteousness,
And the people with his truth.
He will hear the prayer
    of the poor,
And the sighing
    of the prisoner.
He forgives men their sins,
And heals their diseases.
The Lord will abide forever.
    —Adapted from the Psalms

WHEN THINGS GO WRONG

Dear God,
So many things went wrong
    today!
I broke a cup at breakfast,
And on the way to school
I fell and hurt my knee
And tore my new red sweater.
My spelling and arithmetic
Would not come right.
And when I tried to read
    a poem,
I stumbled over all the words,
And spoiled it for my room.

Please help me, God,
To do my best.
And help me
Not to feel too sad
When my mistakes
Pile up so high.

Please help me, God,
And let me know
That you are with me
On the days
When things go wrong.

FOR GOD'S PROTECTION

O God, who loves us,
Keep us, we pray,
From all things
That may hurt us,
And show us the way
That is good for us.

WHOM SHALL I FEAR?

The Lord is my light
And my salvation;
Whom shall I fear?
The Lord is the strength
    of my life;
Of whom shall I be afraid?
—*Psalm 27:1*

FOR THE SICK

O God, who loves all people,
We pray for those
    who are sick.
Fill the doctors with wisdom
And make them skillful.
Let all the sick people,
And all who take care of them,
Feel your love about them.
Let them know of the love
    and thought
Of all who know them
And want to help them.
O God, who loves all people,
Help those who are sick.

MY HELP COMES FROM GOD

My help comes from God,
Who made heaven and earth.
God is my keeper:
He will not slumber nor sleep.
I will rest
And wait for him to help me.
I will trust him and do good.
—*Adapted from the Psalms*

IN THE DAY OF TROUBLE

In the day of trouble
I will call upon you, O God,
For you will answer me.
God is my help and strength,
A very present help
In time of trouble.
Therefore I will not fear.
—*Adapted from the Psalms*

IN DANGER

The wind is blowing strong
Tonight, dear God,
And there is lightning
And thunder in the air.
A tree blew down, and
A window broke with
A crashing noise.
In the time of danger
I will pray to you,
Dear God, and ask you
To take care of me,
And make me brave
And unafraid.

GIVE ME COURAGE

I pray, dear God,
That you will give me courage
When I am in trouble,
Or when I am in danger,
Or when I suffer.
Let me remember Jesus,
Who was not afraid,
But trusted always
        in your love.
Let me trust you, too,
Even when I do not understand.

IN SICKNESS

Dear Father God,
The pain hurts very much.
Please help me to be brave,
But I know you will understand
If I have to cry.
Please help me do
What the doctor says to do,
And not make it harder
For those who take care of me.
And help me, dear God,
To go to sleep
And be better in the morning.

THE LORD'S PRAYER

Our Father who art in heaven,
Hallowed be thy name.
Thy kingdom come,
        thy will be done
On earth, as it is in heaven.
Give us this day our daily bread.
And forgive us our debts
As we forgive our debtors.
And lead us not into temptation,
But deliver us from evil;
For thine is the kingdom,
And the power, and the glory.

IN THE EVENING

BOBBY and Mary were ready for bed. They came to the living room in their pajamas for a good-night talk with their mother and daddy.

"Lots of things have happened today," Bobby said.

"Lots of nice things," Mary remembered. "Daddy fixed my swing for me, and Susan came over to play, and we had a letter from Grandmother, and I wore my new pink dress."

"And Mother made my favorite lemon pie for dinner," Daddy added, giving her a kiss.

"And Mrs. Carroll came to see me," Mother said. "She is so good and kind that she always makes me feel very good and happy, too."

But Bobby was thinking.

"Some bad things happened, too. There was an automobile accident and a man was hurt. And there was a fight at school. And I did not get my arithmetic right."

Daddy made room for him in the big armchair.

"I know, Bobby," he said. "Sad things happen every day

along with the pleasant things. And bad accidents do happen, along with all the wonderful ways doctors have learned to make sick people well. And there are quarrels and fights along with all the goodness and kindness persons show each other. People just do not seem to know how to be good and happy all the time."

Bobby sighed. "I wish everybody could be well and good and happy all the time," he said.

"So do I, son. And God is helping people to learn how to be well and happy and good. If we talk with him about what happens each day, he will forgive us for what we have done wrong. And he will help us to know what we can do to make the next day a good day for everybody who meets us."

Mother and Daddy and Bobby and Mary all watched the fire for a little while, thinking about God and how he helped people.

"We can pray some good-night prayers," Mary said. "I like to say prayers at night. I like to thank God for the nice things that have happened."

"I think talking with God is the very best way to end the day," Mother agreed. "To thank him for the good things and ask his forgiveness for what we have done wrong."

"It is so *good* to know we can pray to God," Daddy said. "We can all go to sleep feeling sure of his love. And knowing he never goes to sleep, but cares for us always."

Bobby nodded. "Yes, it is good to pray before we go to sleep," he said. "It makes me feel happy and safe inside of me. Let's pray now."

And so Mother and Daddy and Mary and Bobby prayed their good-night prayers, and then they went to their beds and slept.

EVENING PRAYERS

THEY THAT WAIT UPON GOD

God, the creator,
Faints not, neither is weary.
They that wait upon the Lord
Shall renew their strength.
They shall mount up
With wings as eagles.
They shall run and not be weary;
They shall walk and not faint.
—*Isaiah 40:28-30*

THE TIME OF SLEEP HAS COME

Dear God, I think of you
As the time of darkness
    and sleep has come.
It makes me rest to know
That all the night through
You will not be asleep
But will be watching over me.
Let me sleep soundly,
Remembering that you made
The night for sleep.
Let my dreams be happy ones,
And if I should wake up,
Let me think again of you.

GOD IS NEAR ME

As the light of sunset fades
And the stars come
    into the evening sky,
Let me know, dear God,
That you are near me.
As the sounds of day die away,
And the quiet night comes on,
Let me know, dear God,
That you are near me.

FOR THE DAY THAT HAS ENDED

All day you have been with me,
    dear God.
You helped me do the things
    I should,
And let me see the loveliness
Of the deeds of kindness done
    by others.
For all the gladness
    and the goodness
That this day has brought,
I thank you,
    dear God.

BE WITH US, LORD

Be with us, Lord,
As we go to sleep.
Let us know we are not alone,
Since you are near.
Be with the sick
And those who are tired,
And comfort them
And give them rest.

THE CHILDREN OF THE WORLD

As I say my evening prayer
I would remember, dear God,
All the children of the world,
And ask your blessing on them all.
Some are hungry,
And some are cold,
And some are lonely and afraid.
Please help them, God.
Show them your love,
And help us all to know
How we may help each other.

GOOD NIGHT

Good night, dear God,.
I'm off to sleep
And in your care, I know.

A QUIET MIND

Give me a quiet mind, O God,
As I lie down to rest.
Be in my thoughts
Until I go to sleep.
Let no bad dreams disturb me,
And let me wake up happy
And ready for a new day.

THANKSGIVING FOR NIGHT

I thank you, God, for night:
For the velvet sky
And the shining stars;
For the quietness that comes
When the day's work is over;
For the gathering of families
In their homes,
Where they may rest
And be with those they love;
For the darkness that comes
When the lights are put out,
And everyone goes to bed;
For rest and peace and sleep,
And the comforting thoughts
Of the love and care of God.
I thank you, God, for the night.

FORGIVE ME, GOD

The day is ended now
And I would talk with you,
    dear God,
Before I go to sleep.
I remember the duties
I have not done,
The cross words I have spoken,
The mean thoughts
That have come to my mind.
I remember the kindness
I might have shown and did not.
I remember how I wanted
    my own way
When another way would
    have been better.
Before I go to sleep,
Forgive me, God, for not doing
What I knew was right.
And when tomorrow comes,
Give me the will to do your will
And follow after what is good.

FOR OUR HOME

O God, our Father,
For our house, our food,
    our health,
For all who serve our home,
We thank you.

For making us dear to
    one another;
For the good times
    we have together;
For Mother, Father,
Brother, Sister,
We thank you.

That you will help us
    every day
To show love and kindness
    to one another,
That each one may think
    of the other
And be ready to share and help,
We pray, dear God, our Father.

THE EARTH IS AT REST

The whole earth
Is at rest and quiet.
It is good for me

To draw near to God.
I will lie down in peace
And sleep.

PRINTED IN U.S.